ANDREW LLOYD WEBBER™

FOR CLASSICAL GUITAR

Music Edited and Arranged by
JOHN ZARADIN and TIM PHILLIPS

Andrew Lloyd Webber™ is a trademark owned by Andrew Lloyd Webber.

ISBN 978-1-4950-9861-1

7777 W. BLUEMOUND RD. P.O. BOX 13819 MILWAUKEE, WI 53213

In Australia Contact:
Hal Leonard Australia Pty. Ltd.
4 Lentara Court
Cheltenham, Victoria, 3192 Australia
Email: ausadmin@halleonard.com.au

Visit Hal Leonard Online at
www.halleonard.com

All I Ask of You

from THE PHANTOM OF THE OPERA

Music by Andrew Lloyd Webber
Lyrics by Charles Hart
Additional Lyrics by Richard Stilgoe

Drop D tuning:
(low to high) D-A-D-G-B-E

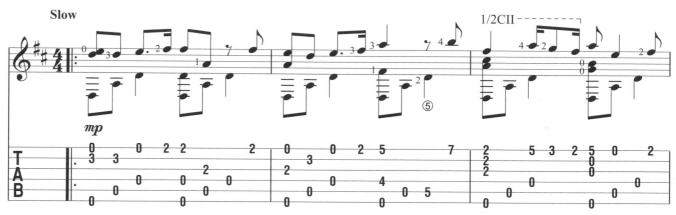

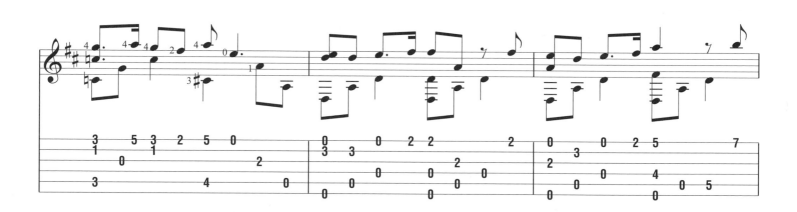

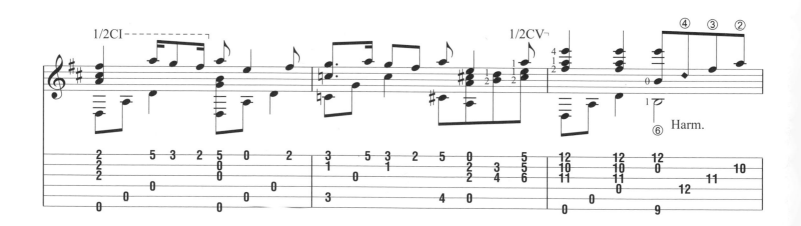

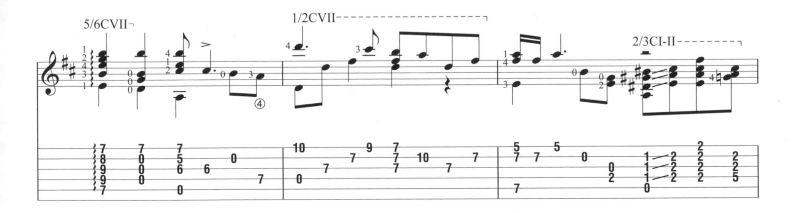

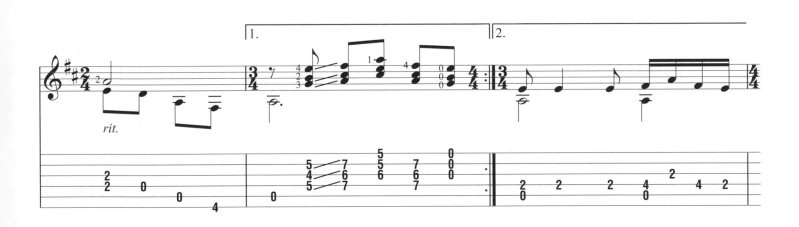

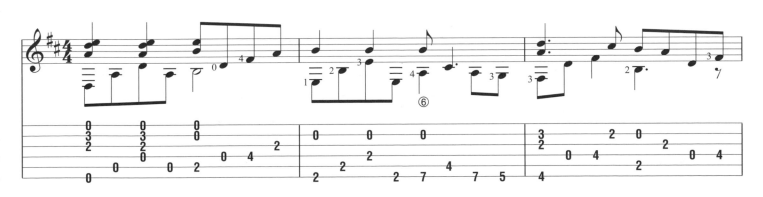

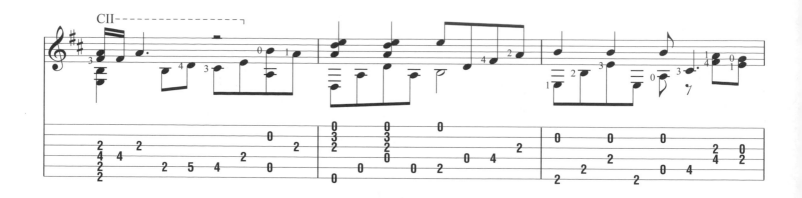

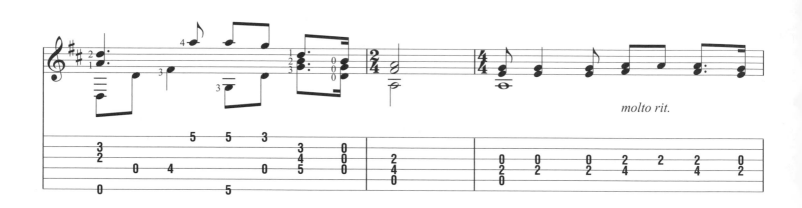

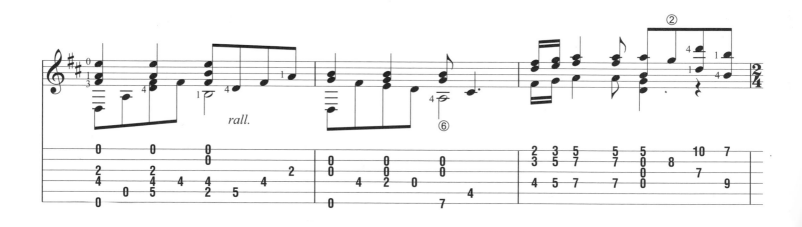

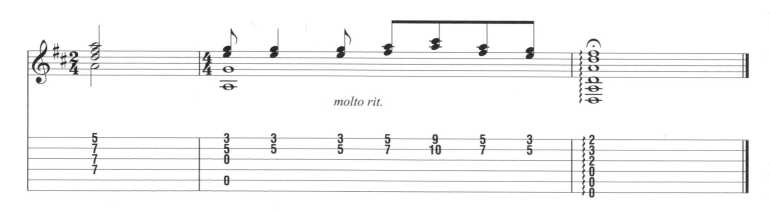

Another Suitcase in Another Hall

from EVITA

Words by Tim Rice
Music by Andrew Lloyd Webber

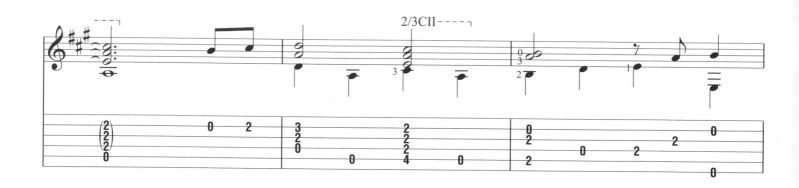

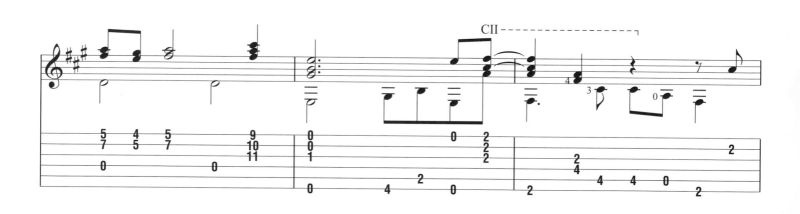

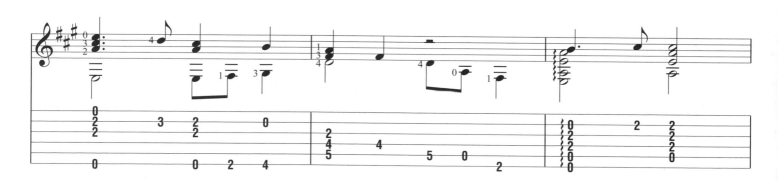

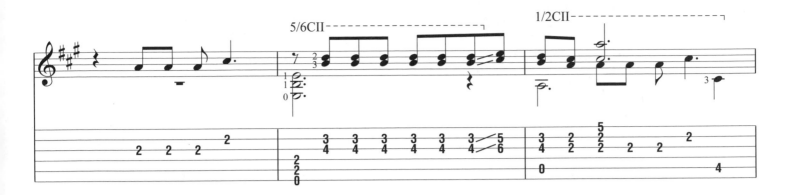

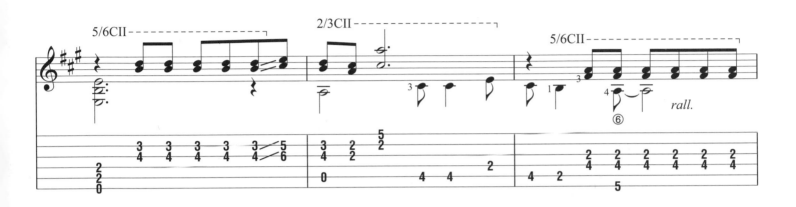

Close Every Door

from JOSEPH AND THE AMAZING TECHNICOLOR® DREAMCOAT

Music by Andrew Lloyd Webber
Lyrics by Tim Rice

Don't Cry for Me Argentina

from EVITA

Words by Tim Rice
Music by Andrew Lloyd Webber

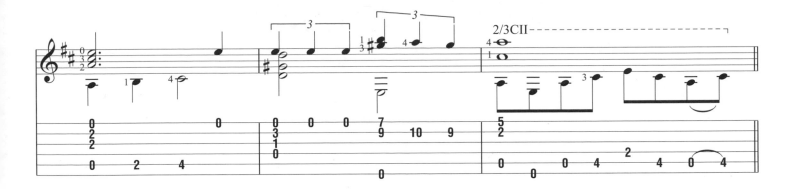

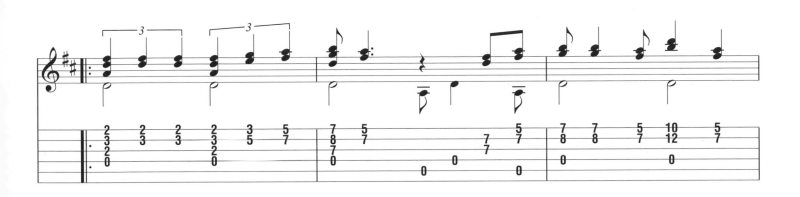

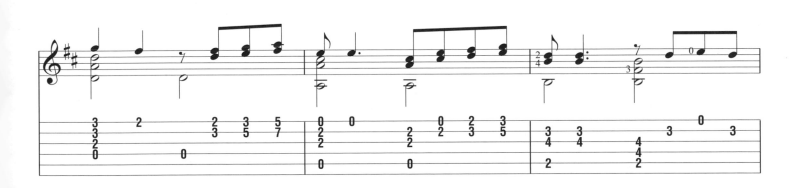

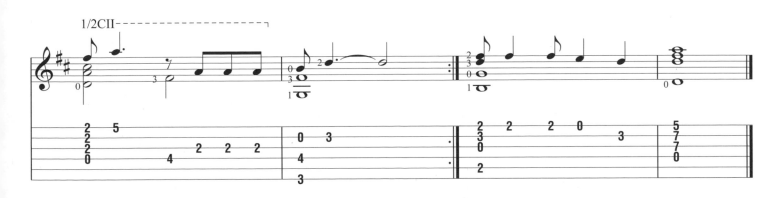

Gus: The Theatre Cat

from CATS

Music by Andrew Lloyd Webber
Text by T. S. Eliot

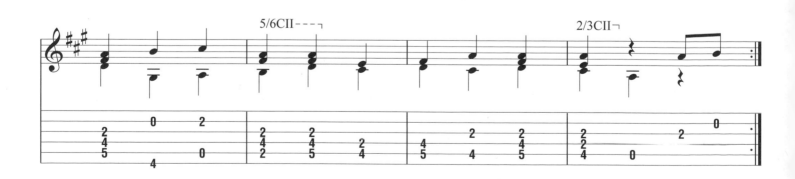

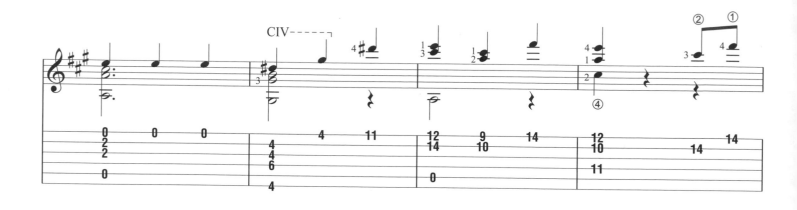

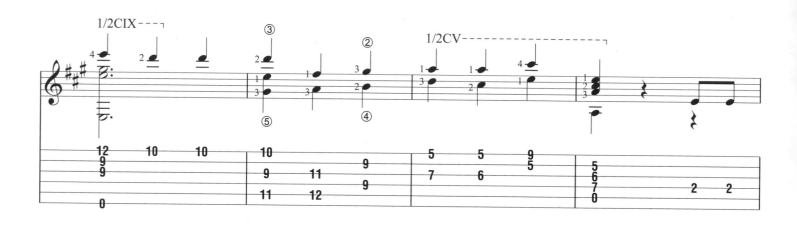

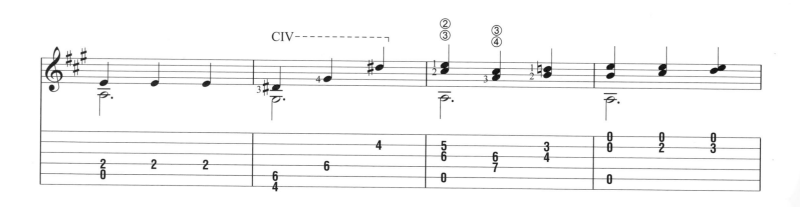

I Don't Know How to Love Him

from JESUS CHRIST SUPERSTAR

Words by Tim Rice
Music by Andrew Lloyd Webber

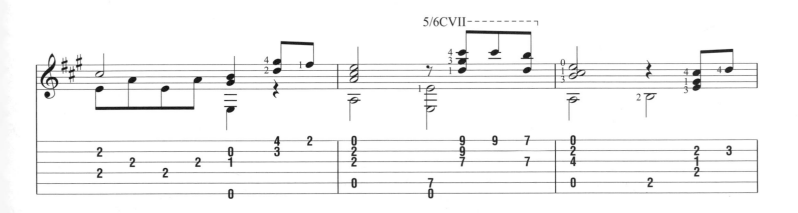

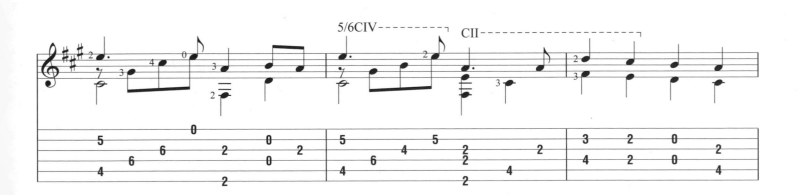

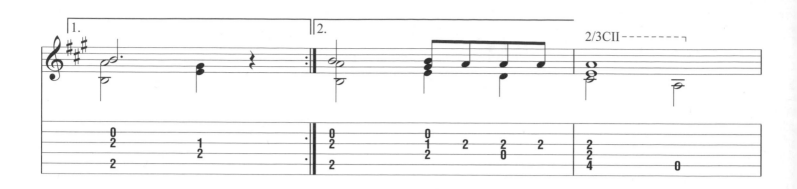

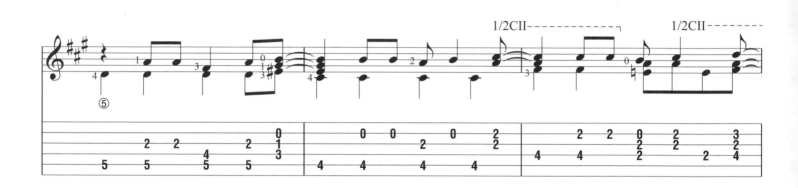

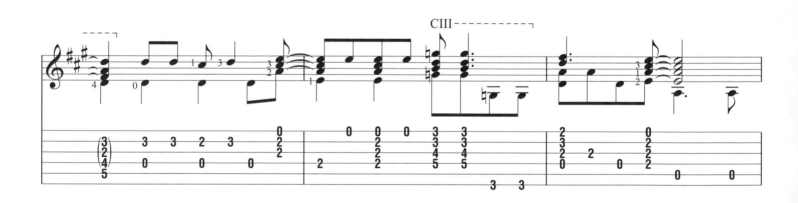

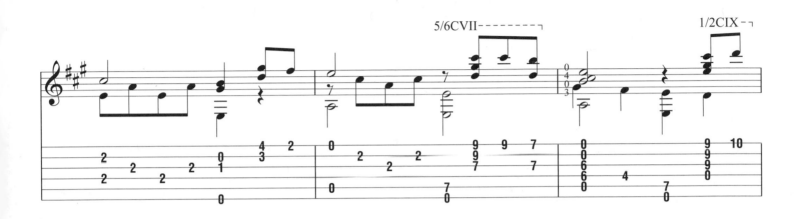

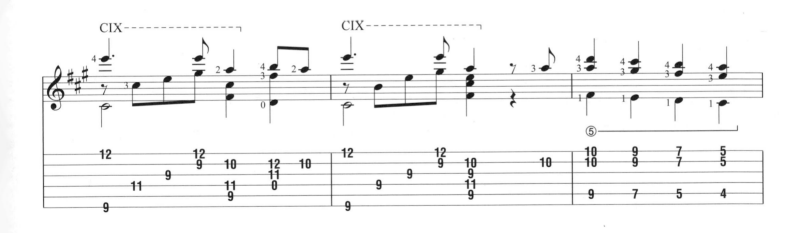

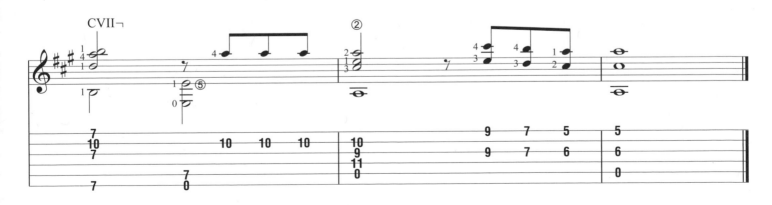

The Last Man in My Life

from SONG & DANCE

Music by Andrew Lloyd Webber
Lyrics by Don Black

Love Changes Everything

from ASPECTS OF LOVE
Music by Andrew Lloyd Webber
Lyrics by Don Black and Charles Hart

Drop D tuning:
(low to high) D-A-D-G-B-E

Moderately

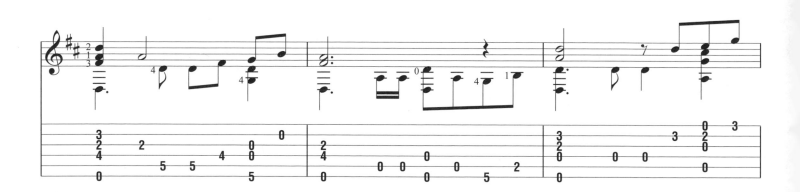

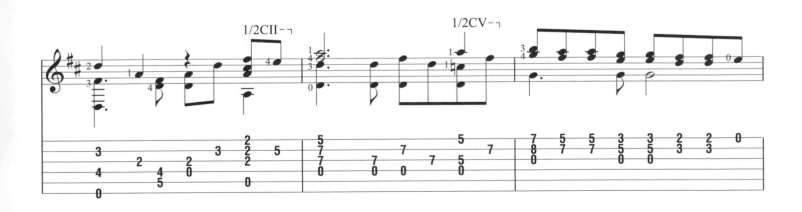

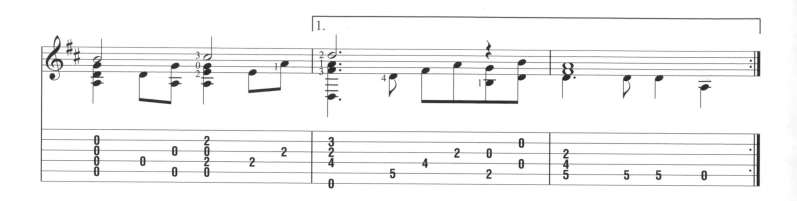

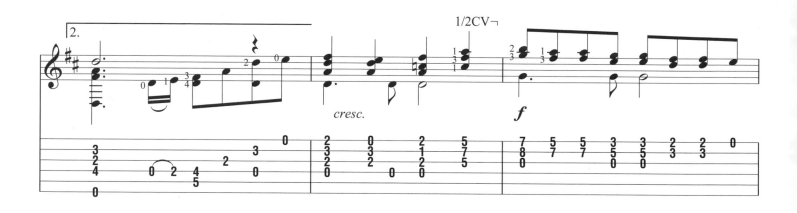

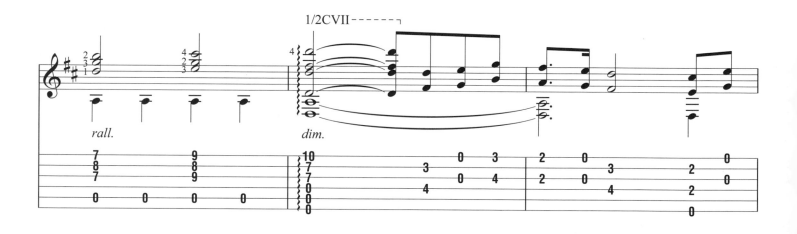

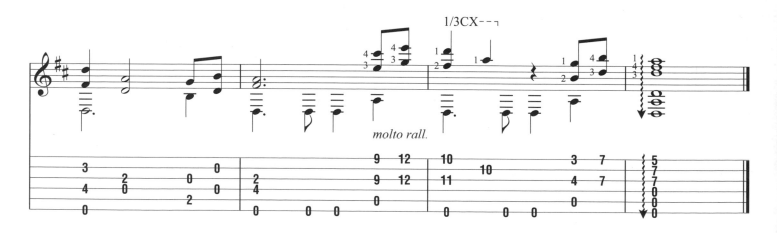

Make Up My Heart

from STARLIGHT EXPRESS
Music by Andrew Lloyd Webber
Lyrics by Richard Stilgoe

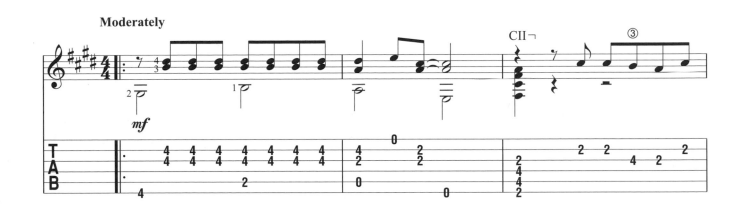

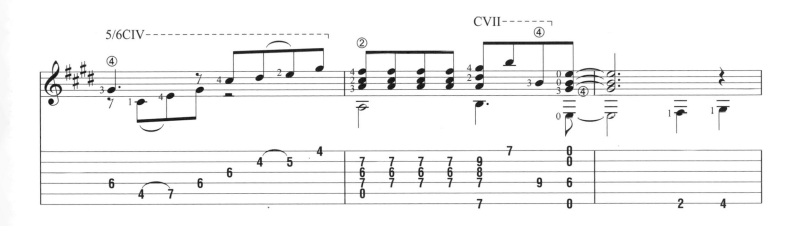

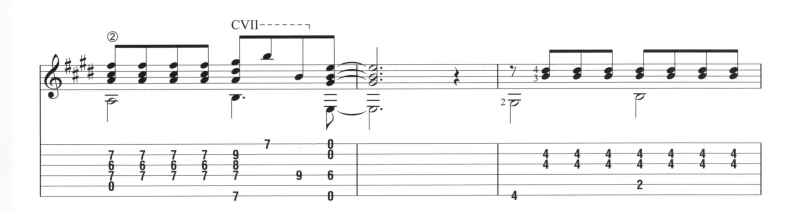

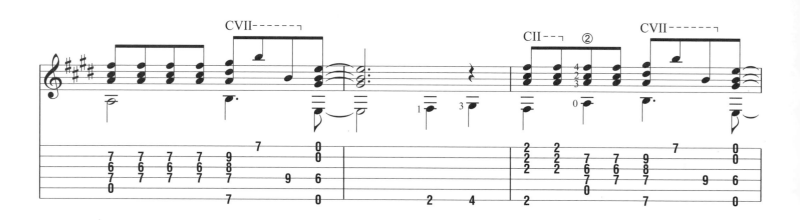

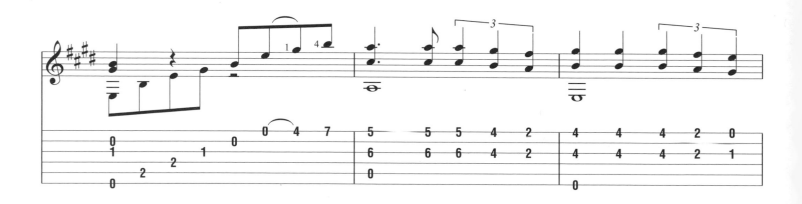

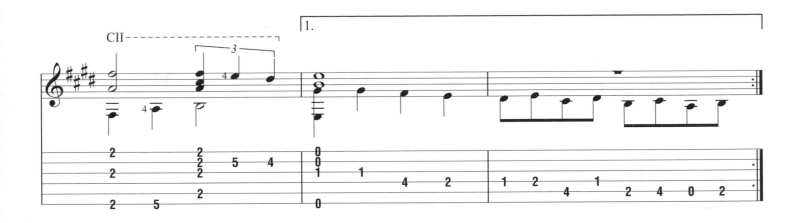

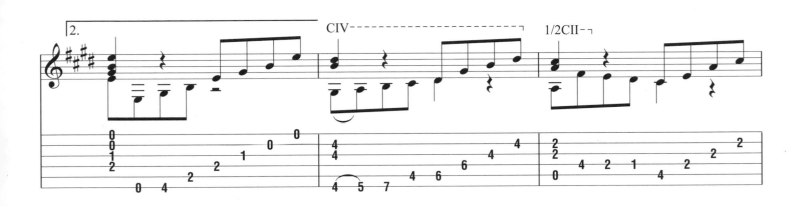

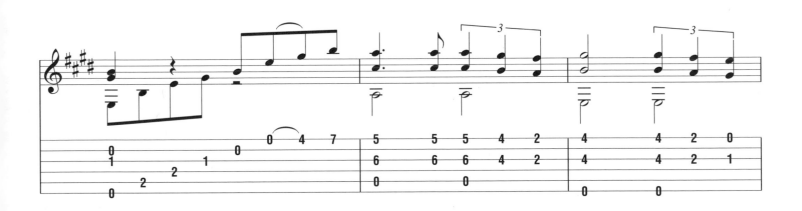

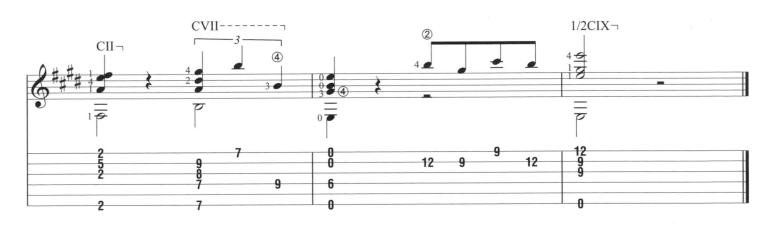

Memory
from CATS
Music by Andrew Lloyd Webber
Text by Trevor Nunn after T. S. Eliot

Slowly, in 4

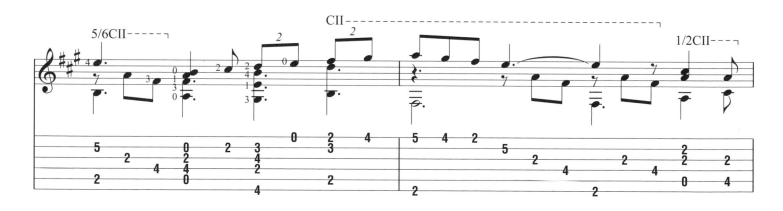

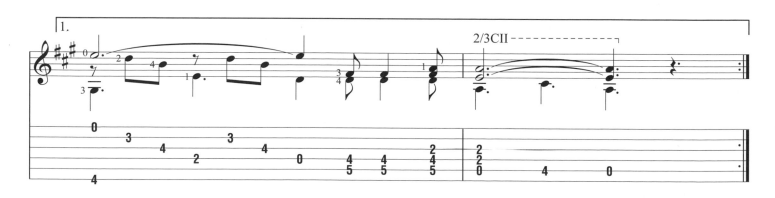

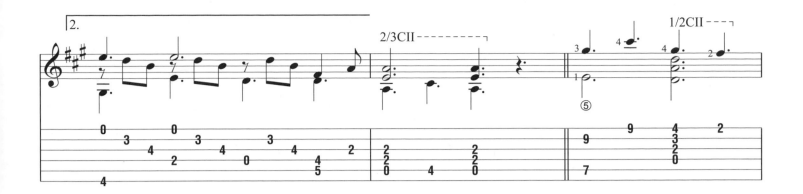

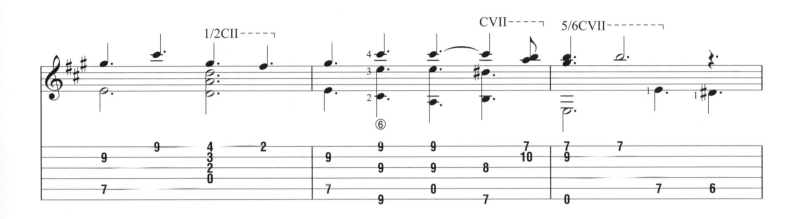

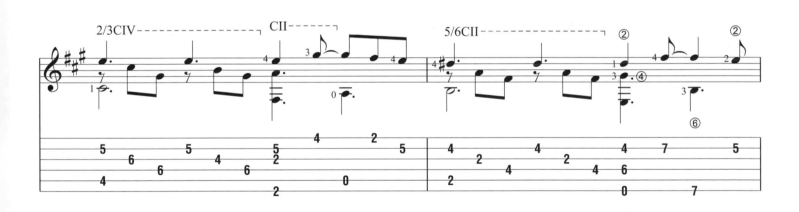

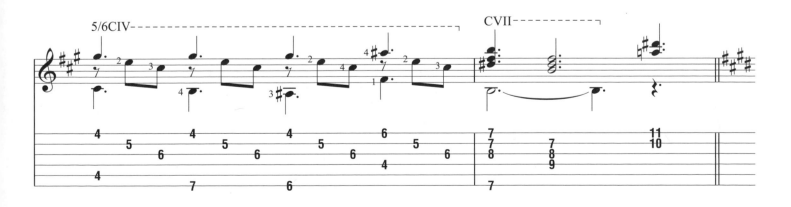

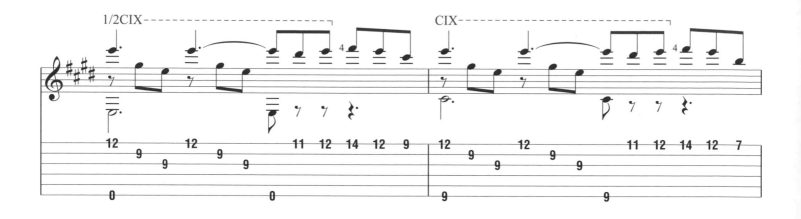

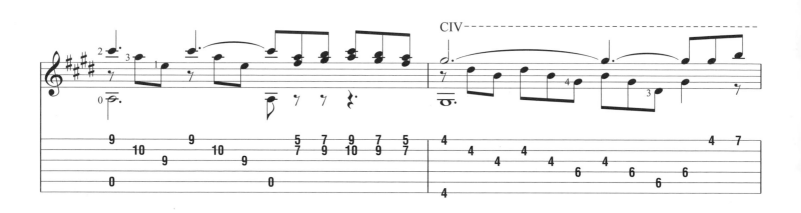

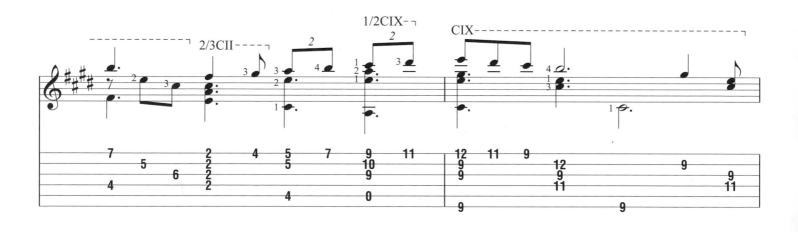

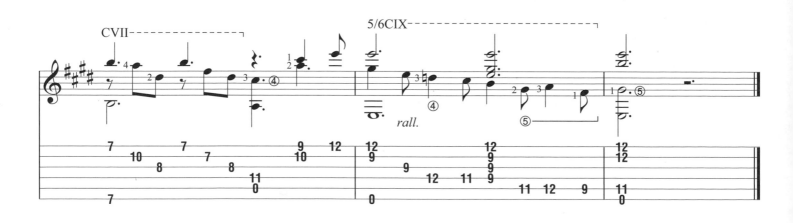

Mr. Mistoffelees

from CATS

Music by Andrew Lloyd Webber
Text by T. S. Eliot

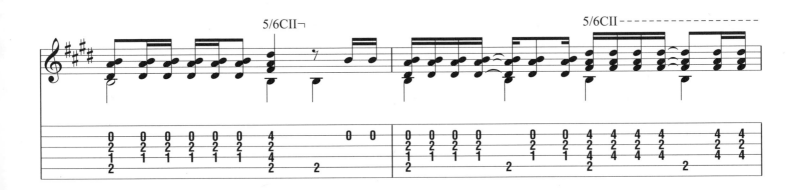

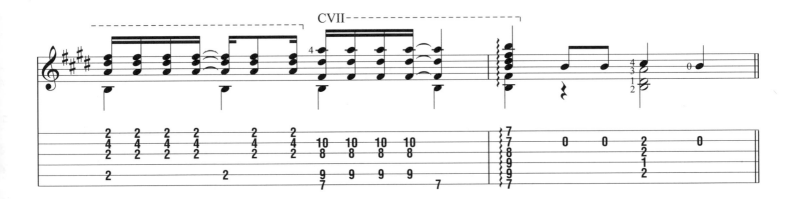

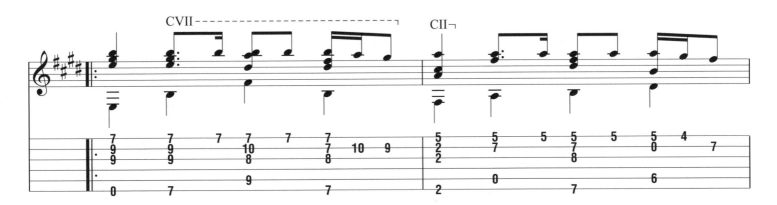

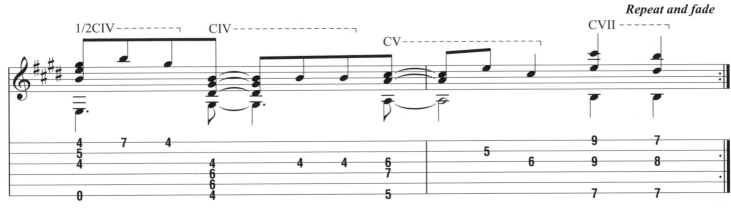

The Music of the Night

from THE PHANTOM OF THE OPERA
Music by Andrew Lloyd Webber
Lyrics by Charles Hart
Additional Lyrics by Richard Stilgoe

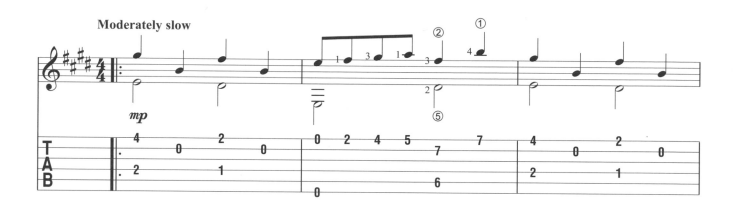

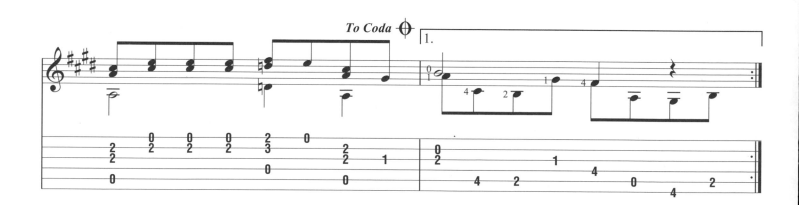

Only You

from STARLIGHT EXPRESS

Music by Andrew Lloyd Webber
Lyrics by Richard Stilgoe

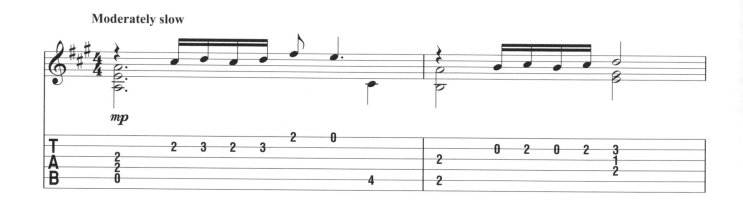

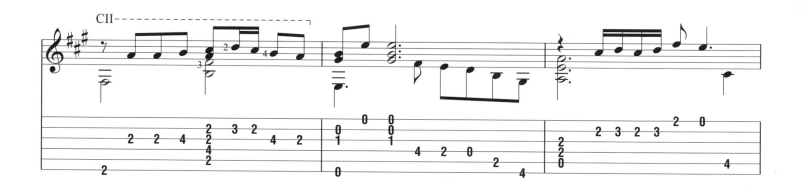

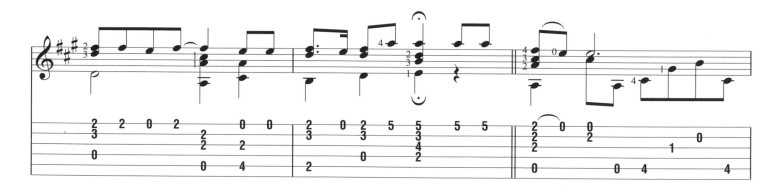

The Phantom of the Opera

from THE PHANTOM OF THE OPERA

Music by Andrew Lloyd Webber
Lyrics by Charles Hart
Additional Lyrics by Richard Stilgoe and Mike Batt

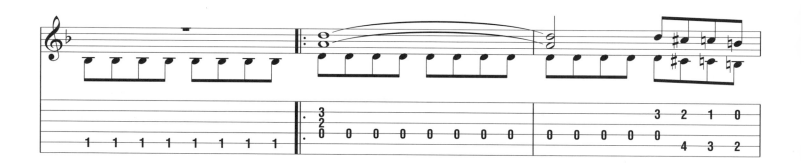

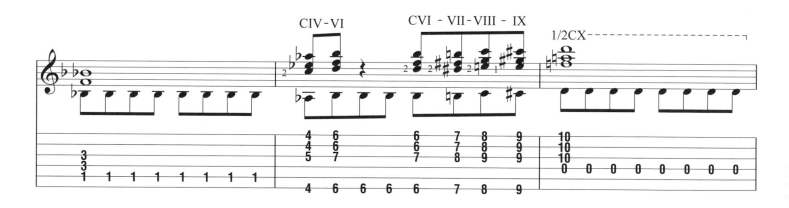

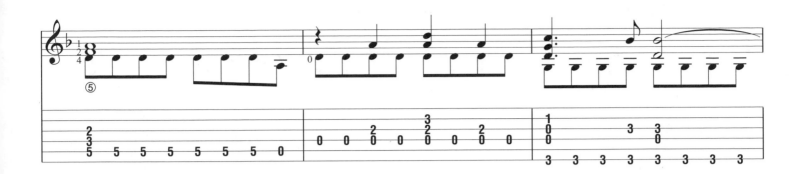

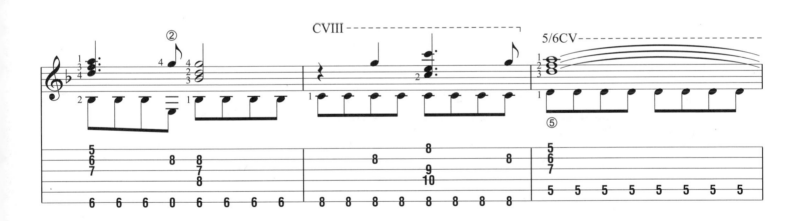

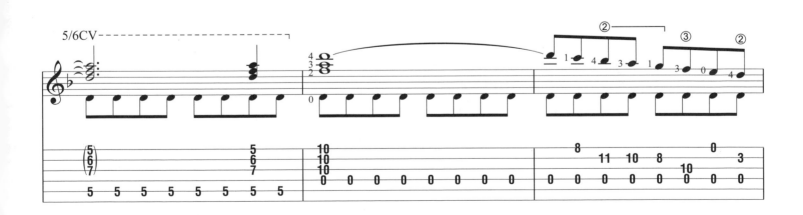

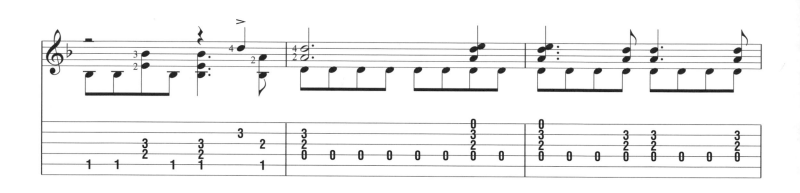

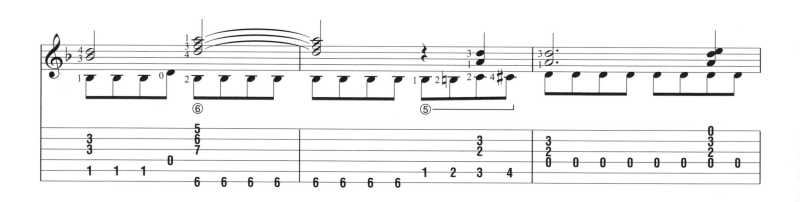

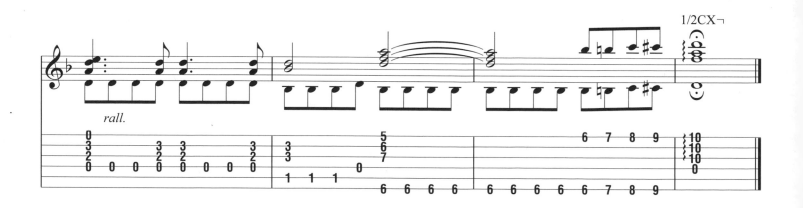

Pie Jesu

from REQUIEM

By Andrew Lloyd Webber

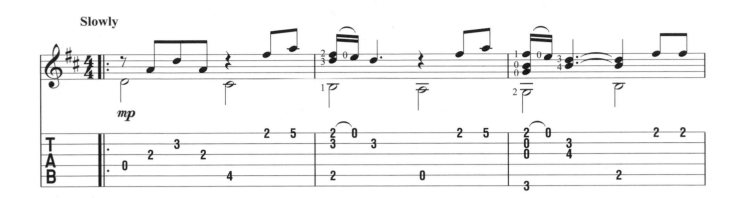

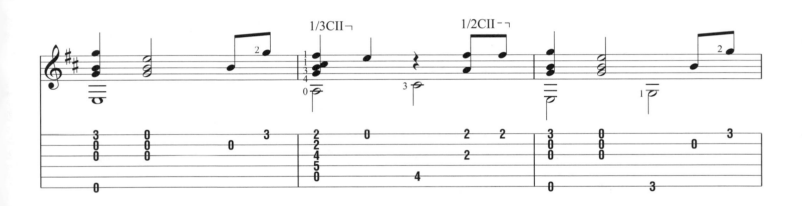

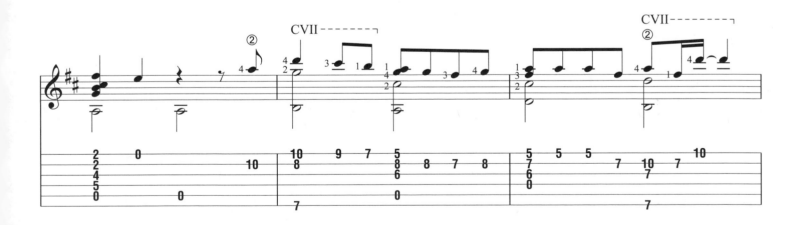

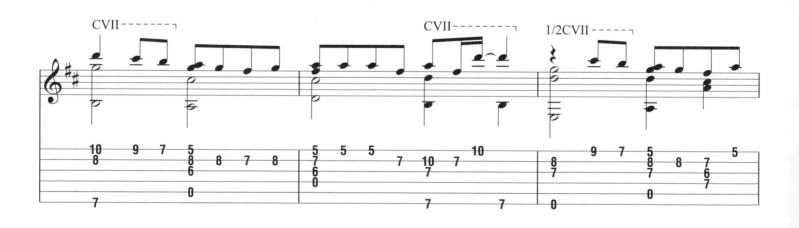

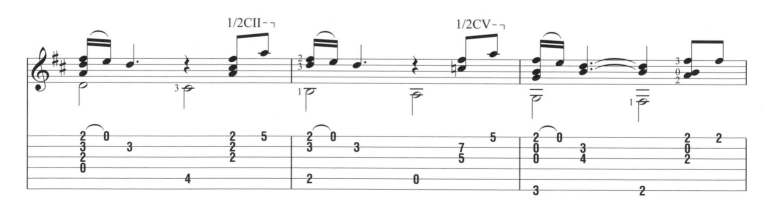

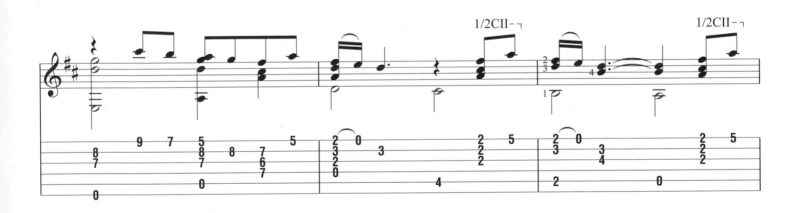

Starlight Express

from STARLIGHT EXPRESS

Music by Andrew Lloyd Webber
Lyrics by Richard Stilgoe

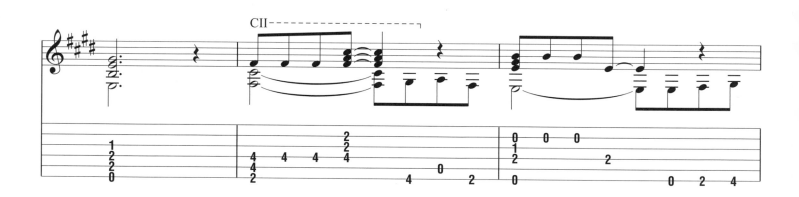

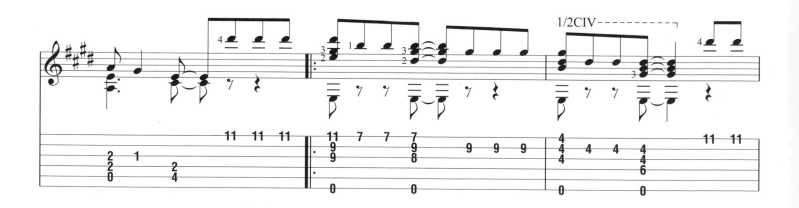

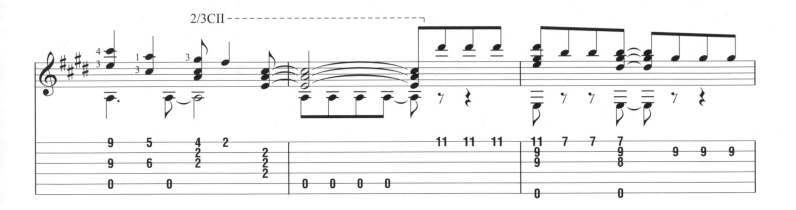

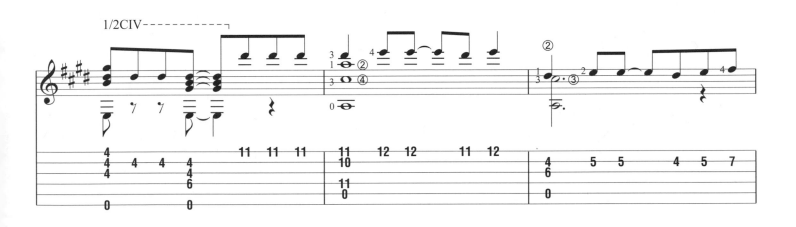

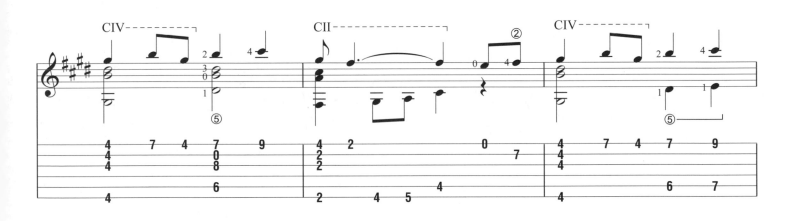

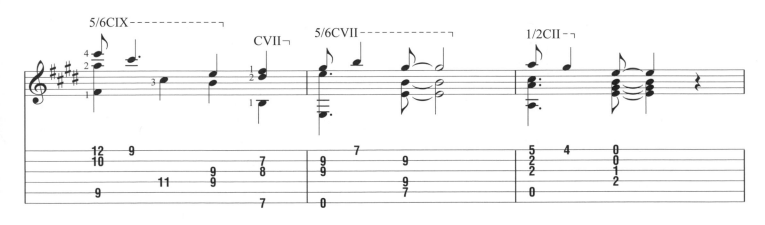

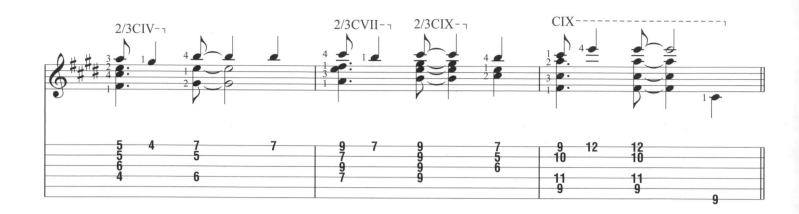

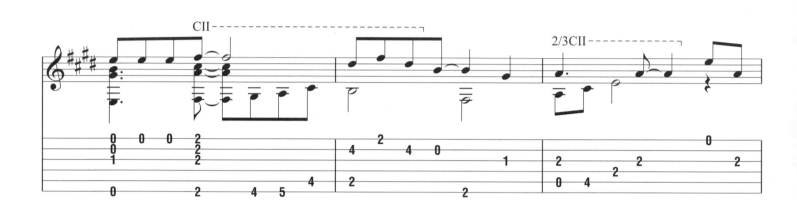

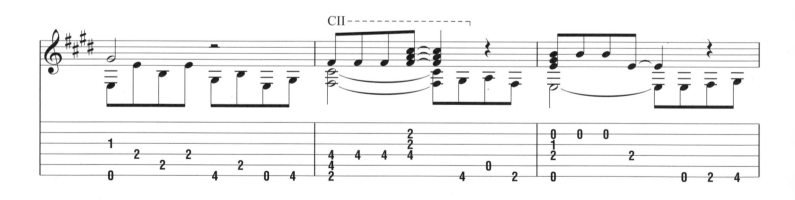

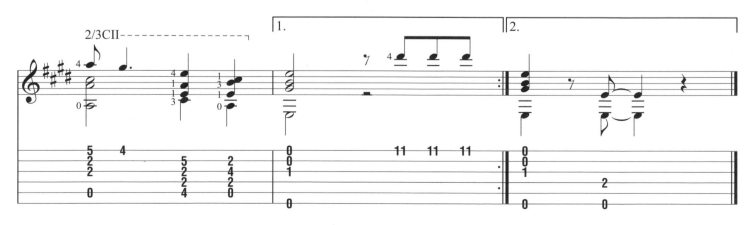

Take That Look Off Your Face

from SONG & DANCE

Music by Andrew Lloyd Webber
Lyrics by Don Black

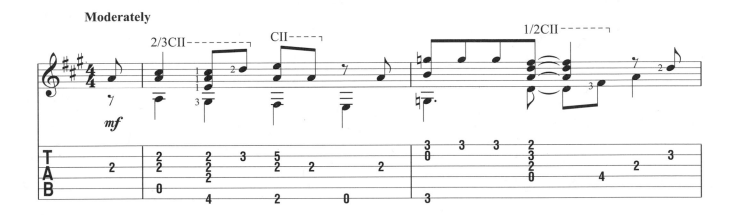

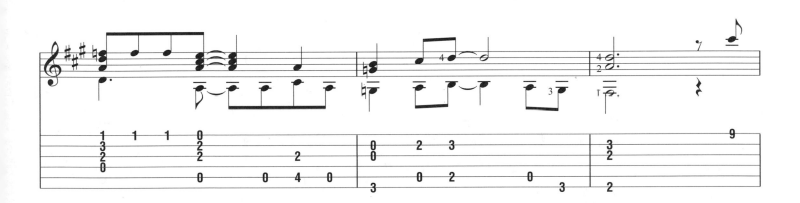

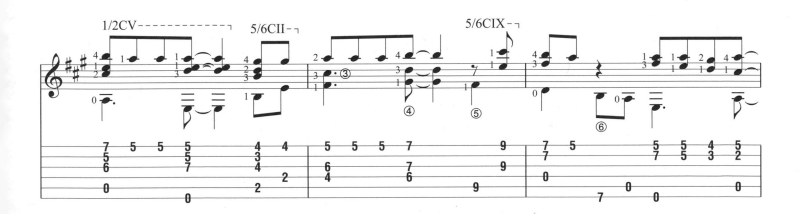

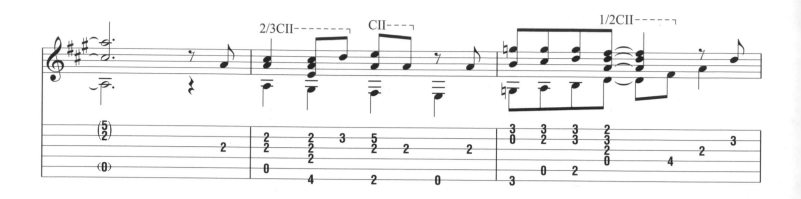

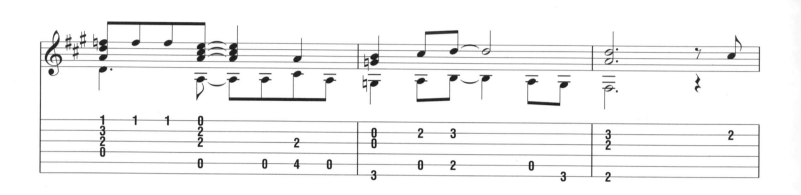

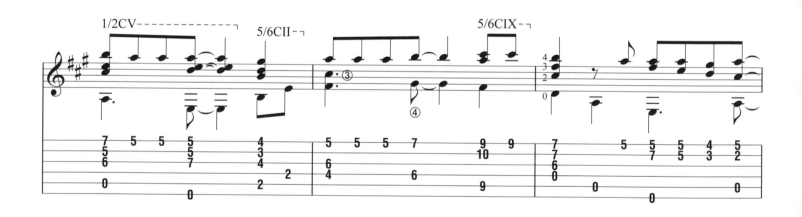

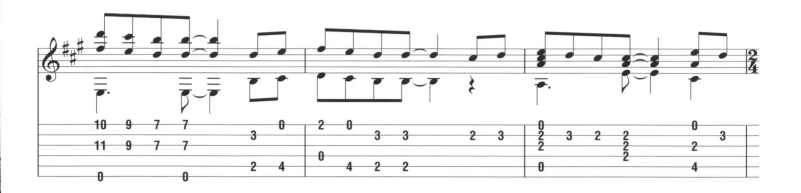

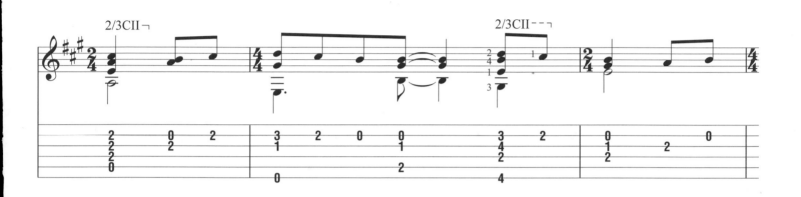

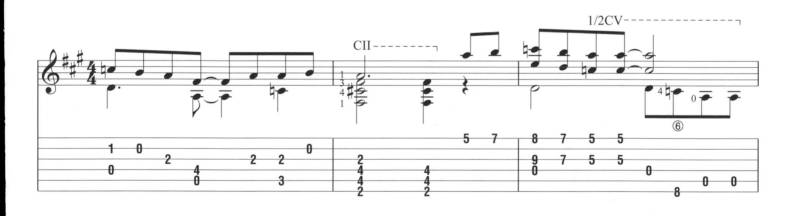

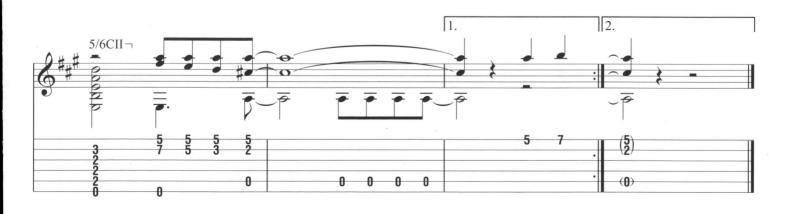

Superstar

from JESUS CHRIST SUPERSTAR
Words by Tim Rice
Music by Andrew Lloyd Webber

Moderately fast

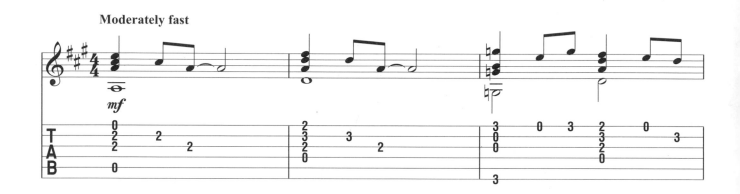

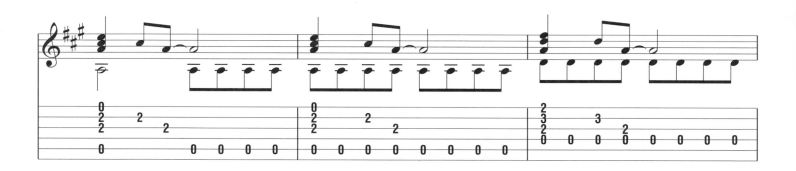

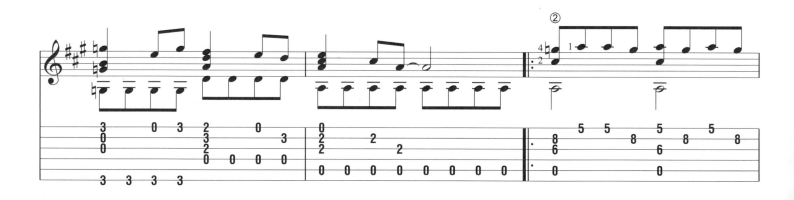

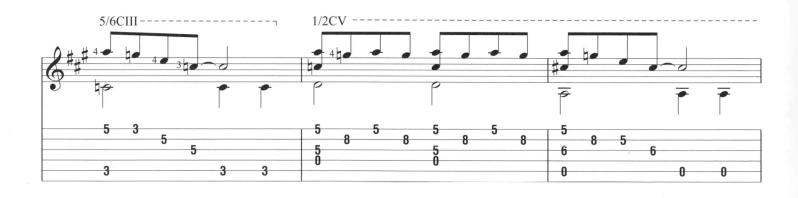

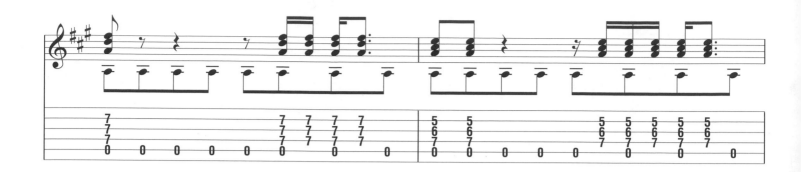

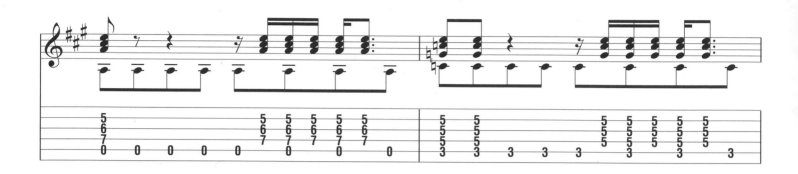

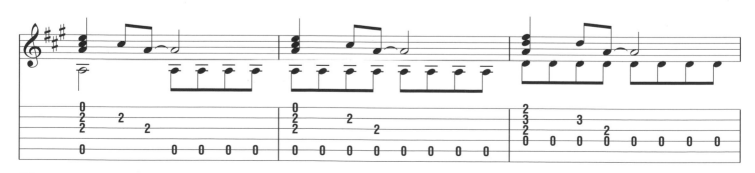

Tell Me on a Sunday

from SONG & DANCE

Music by Andrew Lloyd Webber
Lyrics by Don Black

There's Me

from STARLIGHT EXPRESS

Music by Andrew Lloyd Webber
Lyrics by Richard Stilgoe

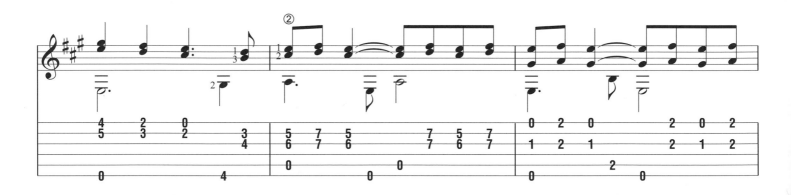

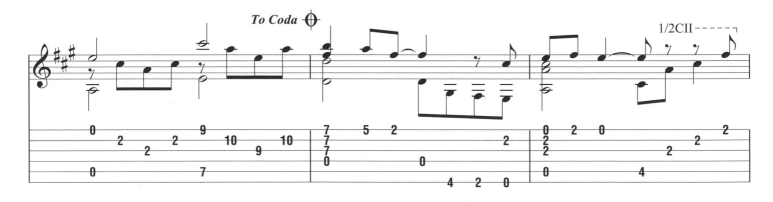

Wishing You Were Somehow Here Again

from THE PHANTOM OF THE OPERA

Music by Andrew Lloyd Webber
Lyrics by Charles Hart
Additional Lyrics by Richard Stilgoe

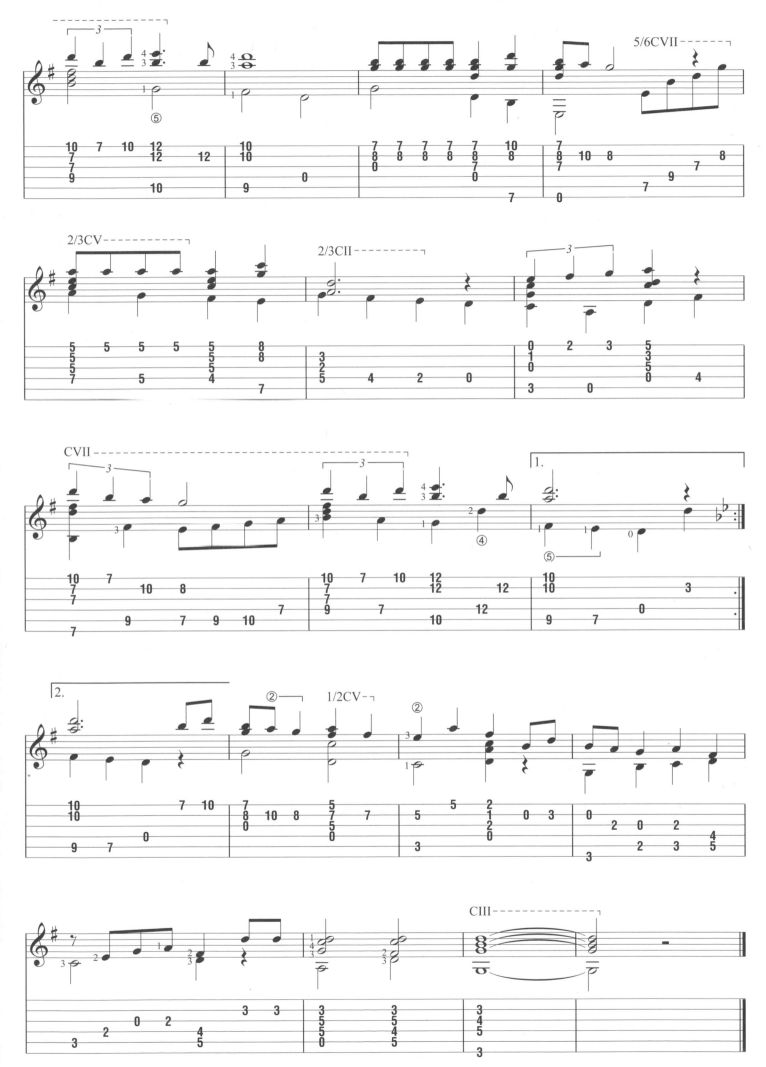

Unexpected Song

from SONG & DANCE
Music by Andrew Lloyd Webber
Lyrics by Don Black

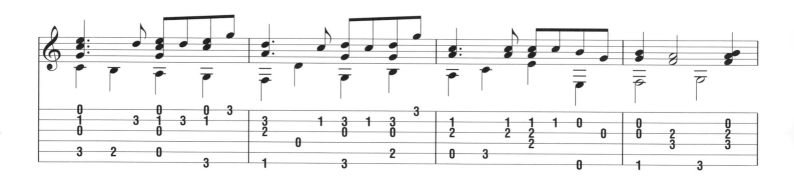

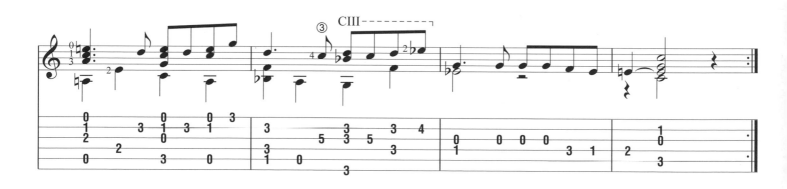

GUITAR NOTATION LEGEND

THE MUSICAL STAFF shows pitches and rhythms and is divided by bar lines into measures. Pitches are named after the first seven letters of the alphabet.

TABLATURE graphically represents the guitar fingerboard. Each horizontal line represents a string, and each number represents a fret.

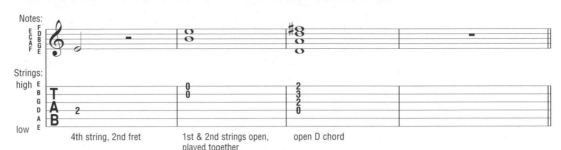

4th string, 2nd fret

1st & 2nd strings open, played together

open D chord

HALF-STEP BEND: Strike the note and bend up 1/2 step.

BEND AND RELEASE: Strike the note and bend up as indicated, then release back to the original note. Only the first note is struck.

HAMMER-ON: Strike the first (lower) note with one finger, then sound the higher note (on the same string) with another finger by fretting it without picking.

TRILL: Very rapidly alternate between the notes indicated by continuously hammering on and pulling off.

TREMOLO PICKING: The note is picked as rapidly and continuously as possible.

WHOLE-STEP BEND: Strike the note and bend up one step.

PRE-BEND: Bend the note as indicated, then strike it.

PULL-OFF: Place both fingers on the notes to be sounded. Strike the first note and without picking, pull the finger off to sound the second (lower) note.

TAPPING: Hammer ("tap") the fret indicated with the pick-hand index or middle finger and pull off to the note fretted by the fret hand.

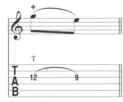

VIBRATO BAR DIVE AND RETURN: The pitch of the note or chord is dropped a specified number of steps (in rhythm), then returned to the original pitch.

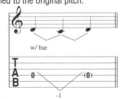

GRACE NOTE BEND: Strike the note and immediately bend up as indicated.

VIBRATO: The string is vibrated by rapidly bending and releasing the note with the fretting hand.

LEGATO SLIDE: Strike the first note and then slide the same fret-hand finger up or down to the second note. The second note is not struck.

NATURAL HARMONIC: Strike the note while the fret-hand lightly touches the string directly over the fret indicated.

VIBRATO BAR SCOOP: Depress the bar just before striking the note, then quickly release the bar.

SLIGHT (MICROTONE) BEND: Strike the note and bend up 1/4 step.

PALM MUTING: The note is partially muted by the pick hand lightly touching the string(s) just before the bridge.

SHIFT SLIDE: Same as legato slide, except the second note is struck.

PINCH HARMONIC: The note is fretted normally and a harmonic is produced by adding the edge of the thumb or the tip of the index finger of the pick hand to the normal pick attack.

VIBRATO BAR DIP: Strike the note and then immediately drop a specified number of steps, then release back to the original pitch.

Additional Musical Definitions

(accent) • Accentuate note (play it louder).

(staccato) • Play the note short.

D.S. al Coda • Go back to the sign (%), then play until the measure marked "***To Coda***," then skip to the section labelled "**Coda**."

D.C. al Fine • Go back to the beginning of the song and play until the measure marked "***Fine***" (end).

Fill • Label used to identify a brief melodic figure which is to be inserted into the arrangement.

N.C. • Harmony is implied.

  • Repeat measures between signs.

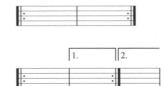 • When a repeated section has different endings, play the first ending only the first time and the second ending only the second time.

CLASSICAL GUITAR

THE BEATLES FOR CLASSICAL GUITAR

Includes 20 solos from big Beatles hits arranged for classical guitar, complete with left-hand and right-hand fingering. Songs include: All My Loving • And I Love Her • Can't Buy Me Love • Fool on the Hill • From a Window • Hey Jude • If I Fell • Let It Be • Michelle • Norwegian Wood • Obla Di • Ticket to Ride • Yesterday • and more. Features arrangements and an introduction by Joe Washington, as well as his helpful hints on classical technique and detailed notes on how to play each song. The book also covers parts and specifications of the classical guitar, tuning, and Joe's "Strata System" – an easy-reading system applied to chord diagrams.
00699237 Classical Guitar $19.99

CZERNY FOR GUITAR

12 SCALE STUDIES FOR CLASSICAL GUITAR
by David Patterson

Adapted from Carl Czerny's *School of Velocity, Op. 299* for piano, this lesson book explores 12 keys with 12 different approaches or "treatments." You will explore a variety of articulations, ranges and technical perspectives as you learn each key. These arrangements will not only improve your ability to play scales fluently, but will also develop your ears, knowledge of the fingerboard, reading abilities, strength and endurance. In standard notation and tablature.
00701248 ....$9.99

MATTEO CARCASSI – 25 MELODIC AND PROGRESSIVE STUDIES, OP. 60

arr. Paul Henry

One of Carcassi's (1792-1853) most famous collections of classical guitar music – indispensable for the modern guitarist's musical and technical development. Performed by Paul Henry. 49-minute audio accompaniment.
00696506 Book/Online Audio $17.99

CLASSICAL & FINGERSTYLE GUITAR TECHNIQUES

by David Oakes • Musicians Institute

This Master Class is aimed at any electric or acoustic guitarist who wants a quick, thorough grounding in the essentials of classical and fingerstyle technique. Topics covered include: arpeggios and scales, free stroke and rest stroke, P-i scale technique, three-to-a-string patterns, natural and artificial harmonics, tremolo and rasgueado, and more. The book includes 12 intensive lessons for right and left hand in standard notation & tab, and the audio features 92 solo acoustic tracks.
00695171 Book/Online Audio $17.99

CLASSICAL GUITAR CHRISTMAS COLLECTION

Includes classical guitar arrangements in standard notation and tablature for more than two dozen beloved carols: Angels We Have Heard on High • Auld Lang Syne • Ave Maria • Away in a Manger • Canon in D • The First Noel • God Rest Ye Merry, Gentlemen • Hark! the Herald Angels Sing • I Saw Three Ships • Jesu, Joy of Man's Desiring • Joy to the World • O Christmas Tree • O Holy Night • Silent Night • What Child Is This? • and more.
00699493 Guitar Solo $10.99

CLASSICAL GUITAR WEDDING

Perfect for players hired to perform for someone's big day, this songbook features 16 classical wedding favorites arranged for solo guitar in standard notation and tablature. Includes: Air on the G String • Ave Maria • Bridal Chorus • Canon in D • Jesu, Joy of Man's Desiring • Minuet • Sheep May Safely Graze • Wedding March • and more.
00699563 Solo Guitar with Tab $12.99

CLASSICAL MASTERPIECES FOR GUITAR

27 works by Bach, Beethoven, Handel, Mendelssohn, Mozart and more transcribed with standard notation and tablature. Now anyone can enjoy classical material regardless of their guitar background. Also features stay-open binding.
00699312 ....$12.95

MASTERWORKS FOR GUITAR

Over 60 Favorites from Four Centuries
World's Great Classical Music

Dozens of classical masterpieces: Allemande • Bourree • Canon in D • Jesu, Joy of Man's Desiring • Lagrima • Malaguena • Mazurka • Piano Sonata No. 14 in C# Minor (Moonlight) Op. 27 No. 2 First Movement Theme • Ode to Joy • Prelude No. I (Well-Tempered Clavier).
00699503 ....$16.95

A MODERN APPROACH TO CLASSICAL GUITAR

by Charles Duncan

This multi-volume method was developed to allow students to study the art of classical guitar within a new, more contemporary framework. For private, class or self-instruction. Book One incorporates chord frames and symbols, as well as a recording to assist in tuning and to provide accompaniments for at-home practice. Book One also introduces beginning fingerboard technique and music theory. Book Two and Three build upon the techniques learned in Book One.
00695114 Book 1 – Book Only $6.99
00695113 Book 1 – Book/Online Audio...............$10.99
00695116 Book 2 – Book Only $6.99
00695115 Book 2 – Book/Online Audio...............$10.99
00699202 Book 3 – Book Only $9.99
00695117 Book 3 – Book/Online Audio...............$12.99
00695119 Composite Book/CD Pack....................$29.99

ANDRES SEGOVIA – 20 STUDIES FOR GUITAR

Sor/Segovia

20 studies for the classical guitar written by Beethoven's contemporary, Fernando Sor, revised, edited and fingered by the great classical guitarist Andres Segovia. These essential repertoire pieces continue to be used by teachers and students to build solid classical technique. Features 50-minute demonstration audio.
00695012 Book/Online Audio $19.99
00006363 Book Only...$7.99

THE FRANCISCO COLLECTION TÁRREGA

edited and performed by Paul Henry

Considered the father of modern classical guitar, Francisco Tárrega revolutionized guitar technique and composed a wealth of music that will be a cornerstone of classical guitar repertoire for centuries to come. This unique book/audio pack features 14 of his most outstanding pieces in standard notation and tab, edited and performed by virtuoso Paul Henry. Includes: Adelita • Capricho Árabe • Estudio Brillante • Grand Jota • Lágrima • Malagueña • María • Recuerdos de la Alhambra • Tango • and more, plus bios of Tárrega and Henry.
00698993 Book/Online Audio $19.99

HAL•LEONARD®

Visit Hal Leonard Online at **www.halleonard.com**

FINGERPICKING GUITAR BOOKS

Hone your fingerpicking skills with these great songbooks featuring solo guitar arrangements in standard notation and tablature. The arrangements in these books are carefully written for intermediate-level guitarists. Each song combines melody and harmony in one superb guitar fingerpicking arrangement. Each book also includes an introduction to basic fingerstyle guitar.

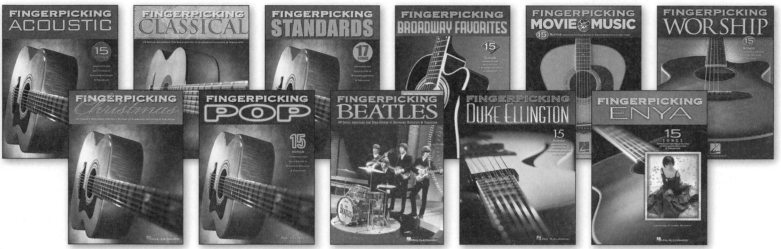

FINGERPICKING ACOUSTIC
00699614...$12.99

FINGERPICKING ACOUSTIC CLASSICS
00160211...$12.99

FINGERPICKING ACOUSTIC HITS
00160202...$12.99

FINGERPICKING ACOUSTIC ROCK
00699764...$12.99

FINGERPICKING BACH
00699793...$10.99

FINGERPICKING BALLADS
00699717...$10.99

FINGERPICKING BEATLES
00699049...$19.99

FINGERPICKING BEETHOVEN
00702390...$7.99

FINGERPICKING BLUES
00701277 ....$9.99

FINGERPICKING BROADWAY FAVORITES
00699843...$9.99

FINGERPICKING BROADWAY HITS
00699838...$7.99

FINGERPICKING CELTIC FOLK
00701148...$10.99

FINGERPICKING CHILDREN'S SONGS
00699712...$9.99

FINGERPICKING CHRISTIAN
00701076 ....$7.99

FINGERPICKING CHRISTMAS
00699599...$9.99

FINGERPICKING CHRISTMAS CLASSICS
00701695...$7.99

FINGERPICKING CHRISTMAS SONGS
00171333...$9.99

FINGERPICKING CLASSICAL
00699620...$10.99

FINGERPICKING COUNTRY
00699687...$10.99

FINGERPICKING DISNEY
00699711...$14.99

FINGERPICKING DUKE ELLINGTON
00699845...$9.99

FINGERPICKING ENYA
00701161...$9.99

FINGERPICKING FILM SCORE MUSIC
00160143...$12.99

FINGERPICKING GOSPEL
00701059...$9.99

FINGERPICKING GUITAR BIBLE
00691040 ....$19.99

FINGERPICKING HIT SONGS
00160195...$12.99

FINGERPICKING HYMNS
00699688...$9.99

FINGERPICKING IRISH SONGS
00701965...$9.99

FINGERPICKING JAZZ FAVORITES
00699844...$7.99

FINGERPICKING JAZZ STANDARDS
00699840...$10.99

FINGERPICKING LATIN FAVORITES
00699842...$9.99

FINGERPICKING LATIN STANDARDS
00699837...$12.99

FINGERPICKING ANDREW LLOYD WEBBER
00699839...$12.99

FINGERPICKING LOVE SONGS
00699841...$12.99

FINGERPICKING LOVE STANDARDS
00699836 ....$9.99

FINGERPICKING LULLABYES
00701276...$9.99

FINGERPICKING MOVIE MUSIC
00699919...$10.99

FINGERPICKING MOZART
00699794...$9.99

FINGERPICKING POP
00699615...$12.99

FINGERPICKING POPULAR HITS
00139079...$12.99

FINGERPICKING PRAISE
00699714...$9.99

FINGERPICKING ROCK
00699716...$10.99

FINGERPICKING STANDARDS
00699613...$12.99

FINGERPICKING WEDDING
00699637...$9.99

FINGERPICKING WORSHIP
00700554...$9.99

**FINGERPICKING NEIL YOUNG –
GREATEST HITS**
00700134...$14.99

FINGERPICKING YULETIDE
00699654...$9.99

HAL•LEONARD®

Visit Hal Leonard online at **www.halleonard.com**

Prices, contents and availability
subject to change without notice.

1217